D1453149

Reason is Powerless
in the
Expression of Love

Volume I

Reshad Feild

Reason is Powerless
in the
Expression of Love

Volume I

Reshad Feild

Chalice Guild

9/03

Set in Baskerville
by WRWebb Associates
Los Angeles, CA.

Printed in the United States.

ISBN 0-9625412-0-6

Acknowledgements

I would like to thank the following people whose sincere efforts made this book possible:

Preparation of transcript:
Sandra Houser, Richard Rozsa,
Nicoli Bailey, Tony Stanton,
Jonathan Yurkanis

Design: *Judy Vogt*
Cover: *Cheryl Southern Smith*
Type: *W.R. Webb*

Bruce Miller
Editor

Contents

Preface

It was 1974, Los Angeles. The "Festival of Light," a non-stop smorgasbord of psychics, astrologers, fruitarians, and feelgooders, all reveling in the collective catharsis known as the "new age." We were a chosen people, destined to erase the memory of Richard Nixon and the Vietnam tragedy with a nostalgia for the future — an Aquarian future, guaranteed to arrive via a cosmic timetable. Just jump aboard; what could be easier?

As speaker after speaker invited the audience to join in his or her personal experience, I began to sense that this spiritual phenomenon was exceedingly narcissistic.

The sentimentality was making me feel vaguely uncomfortable, yet I was drawn to this event by my own deep yearning and questioning about the purpose of life. As a small child, I was once awakened from my sleep with a sense of deep question pulling at me — "What is outside the universe?" In that flash of awe and wonder, as I lay in bed, the melodrama of life made no sense. What is this stage onto which our life plays its role? My mother comforted me and told me to go back to sleep. I didn't.

The next festival speaker was a rather obscure Englishman without any descriptive label after his name on the program. Out stepped a bald and bearded gentleman wearing a fur-lined vest and holding two whalebone dowsing rods. I had noticed him earlier in the hallway demonstrating to a young woman how the rods would bend upwards toward his heart. Curious, indeed. His name was Reshad Feild.

As he spoke, the sound of his voice was free from the sentimentality I had come to accept as "being spiritual." So clear, so direct, shockingly ordinary! Yet, his straightforward manner carried a passion that resounded at the core of my being. "Dare we step outside of time to sacrifice our lives in order to build a platform for the Second Cycle of Mankind?" How petty my self-centered perspective seemed in contrast to the grand cycles of human destiny. A deep reawakening of the responsibility and birthright of being human surged within — there was no turning back. Reshad offered to start a school in Los Angeles, but cautioned that we would have to do all the work. I signed my name.

Thus was born the Institute for Conscious Life, a forty-day experiment to which pupils traveled from all parts of the U.S., Canada, Mexico, and England. It was only after the third week, while linked arm in arm sounding Arabic zikr, that it dawned on me that this school was connected to Sufism, which has its roots in Islam. "So what's a good Jewish boy doing in a place like this?" I asked my perplexed self. Yes, I had made a commitment to Truth, and now I found myself seated in a zikr circle. I promised myself not to identify with the religious form and continued sounding the prayers.

I discovered that the Sufi way is not involved with form. Sufi comes from the root word *suf* which means "wool" and from *saf* which means "pure and adaptable like water." The living roots of my own religious heritage were being awakened through the Sufi tradition.

Needless to say, the school lasted more than forty days. Over the years the school has appeared with various names, with different degrees of form and formlessness, in different cities, different continents, and with an ever-changing cast of characters. The full drama of life has passed through its doors. At one point or another, Reshad has incorporated the teachings of Sufism, Islam, Christianity, Judaism, Buddhism, Zoroastrianism, the Gurdjieff work, Caucasian yoga, and even regimens from the Royal Navy.

Yet, paradoxically, the school has never become eclectic, nor has the integrity of one tradition been sacrificed at the expense of another. Throughout the years, a continuity has emerged founded on the uncompromising affirmation of Unity and a receptivity to the need of the moment.

The articles in this book are the product of the school. Many of the essays were written recently for this book. Others were transcribed from talks given by Reshad. The chapters follow major themes of the school to form an introduction for the student of the Way. The prayers and poems have been included so that the book serves as a devotional resource as well as an informative work.

Taken all together, the essays, poems, and prayers form a picture of a school that is the fusion of passion and knowledge, love and sacrifice, mysticism and common sense. This book is the product of that love — and that sacrifice. I hope that the message it carries helps to bring you to your own beginning.

Bruce Miller
Atlanta, GA
April 15, 1990

Introduction

There are a thousand and one books published on the subject of our life's journey. The spiritual "supermarket" is big business. At the International Book Fair in Frankfurt, Germany, over 8,000 booksellers ply their wares under one roof. The energy is truly amazing, and it is difficult to know where to start looking for a book that will help us through this difficult labyrinth that we call "Life."

There is one very interesting thing to remember in such an event as the Book Fair. With all the hundreds of thousands of titles, and the many different subjects that are offered to the prospective reader, there is one thing that every person has in common, whoever they are and wherever they come from. That is the element of air. Every single person walking past those endless booths is breathing the same air. What an extraordinary awakening that could be if everyone realized this fact at the same time. I wonder just how many people do stop for a moment, at least to consider this, for surely it is what happens to the air after it enters our body and then is sent out into the world on the out-breath that really counts. Breath is life. So often we are told this. And life is both a mystery and a responsibility to be considered at the same time.

So, with all these different books available I still felt that there was room on the shelves for one more contribution. This is a book that the reader can open at random whenever he or she wishes. I hope that something useful will appear from one of the pages to act as a signpost along the Way. Maybe it will be in the spaces between the words that an answer can be found, just as in those rare moments when we stop thinking and a vast space of possibility opens up in front of us. Like the air we breathe, it is what we do with the endlessness that lies behind and within the words that really counts.

Luckily there are schools and teachers in the living tradition of Truth. I hope that all sincere seekers on the Way will be guided, step by step, to come to the Road that leads to Love.

Reshad Feild
January 9th, 1990
Zurich, Switzerland

Part One

Come, Come whoever you are,

Wanderer, worshipper, lover of leaving,

It doesn't matter.

Ours is not a caravan of despair.

Come, even if you have broken your vow

a thousand times.

Come, yet again, come, come.

REASON IS POWERLESS
in the Expression of Love
Reshad Feild

A great shaykh in Turkey once said to me, "The world is full of your prayers. Now all we need is love." I used to wonder about the meaning of these words and it was many years before I understood that for real change to come about in the world we must know the meaning of love — of conscious love. We have to have the knowledge of love, the knowledge of God — for God is love. And yet, without knowledge how can we actually know this?

The shaykh said, "All we need is love." In countries where everyone begins their search already having accepted completely the unity of God, the need for real knowledge is understood. But here in the Western world where so much has been forgotten in man's greed and ignorance, in his incessant search for money and power, people talk about love in such a vague way that it means almost nothing. Here we talk about love and yet we continue to walk the streets like sleepwalkers, hardly ever waking up to the real world which is a world of love. It is a world in which lies the knowledge of love — of pure light and perfect order. It is not a world of chaos, as we see ours is today.

Ralph Waldo Emerson said, "Woe unto him who suffers himself to be betrayed by Fate." Yet mankind accepts this fate with its ebb and tide as a birthright and as an opportunity for self-satisfaction without any obligation in return. We have an inherent obligation in being born, and that is to work in order to know ourselves. We find the real world through the understanding of our responsibility in being born man and woman — the response that comes out of the greater will of God, not just the chaos that comes out of trying to follow our own little wills at the expense of the whole. It is not hard to see where this has led us, is it? Can we not see what has happened already? It is not hard to look around — if we can actually face waking up — and see the results of our own stupidity and willfulness.

Real change is necessary in our world, not just the apparency of change. For real change to come about, the love we talk about so glibly must become conscious love. We must learn to love consciously, and that means we must know who and what we are. How can "I" or "you" say that we love if we do not know that the moment we say "I love," we bring into play, a force which has its own job to do in the universe, regardless of ours, and we are lucky if we do not get hurt in the process. This force of which I speak is the greatest force there is. It comes to help us if we understand it, but it may burn us if we fail to recognize it.

Do you remember the old saying, "Hell hath no fury like a woman scorned"? A woman scorned is a woman who is not recognized for what she is. Sooner or later the frustration and

suppressed anger within her is liable to blow —
to burst out shouting, "Look, look at me you
idiots! For God's sake, look! I can give you
everything, yet you will not see me. You will not
recognize me."

When we say, "I love...I love," whatever that
"I" is, that great force which wishes to help us
comes instantaneously into play and for a while
it is possible things will seem easy for us. But
without knowledge of that force, sooner or later
in its desire for recognition which ultimately
leads to redemption, it is liable to turn around
and woe betide us if we are not in control, not
awake, not conscious.

Yet, there is a paradox in all these things. It
is not possible to know who and what we are,
and therefore have the possibility of the knowledge of the love of God, with the mind. The
mind cannot know these things. Mind cannot
understand what I am talking about. The mind
is not capable of understanding Unity. And God
is One. The mind lives only through comparison — comparison is both its food and its moti-
vation. The mind must compare if it is to exist
at all; but in the real world, the world of love
and order, there is no comparison and thus
there is no fighting, no ignorance, no dishar-
mony. There is peace in perfect order. There is
peace in knowledge — for if you consider it,
nothing else is satisfactory in the end.

So how can we come about the knowledge of
which I speak if not with mind and discursive
reasoning? Is there a way which will lead us

ultimately to our goal — the making of a new world here on earth? Yes, there is a way. It is the path of service and surrender. It is the path of sacrifice. To come upon what is called "The Way" which leads to freedom in fulfilling our obligation in being born here on planet earth, it is necessary that we give up all the concepts we have previously held as to what we thought we wanted or what we felt we needed. We have to give up all ideas of self-development or spiritual attainment. We have to break our concepts on the stone of truth once and for all, and so, finally start on our real journey as travelers on the Way.

The Sufis are called *selik* — travelers, and yet we do not become travelers until we know that to which we aspire. We do not become travelers until we at least give all our heart towards our journey's end. A selik is a man who knows what he is looking for.

On the path of service there is nothing to be gained for "us," who we thought we were when we started to search for our true identity. There is nothing in it for "us" at all. We have to go on surrendering to the will of God every moment of our lives — to give up all that we considered to be real, so that, little by little, delusions are dissolved away and what remains is the knowledge of our essential unity with God.

It is what the Sufis call *fana* and *baka*. *Fana*, the dissolving and the melting of that which is transient and *baka*, the remaining of the permanent "I" which is no more separate from God.

With each moment of surrender, that which can lead us astray is redeemed into eternity, and what remains is the order that must be brought into our world.

This order can lead the world out of chaos into a new age — the second cycle of mankind. Men and women will once more live upon the earth in the knowledge of the meaning of love, for they will have become real human beings at last — God-conscious men and women, awake all the time to the real world, participating consciously in what we call "the Divine plan." They will have become conscious lovers. They will know at last the meaning of Love.

Love without knowledge is not enough. We must see the knowledge beyond the mind that bursts through us as a flash of insight, burning out the illusions in our yearning to know the Truth. We are asked to come upon this knowledge, not by seeking it elsewhere, not by chasing moonbeams, but by surrendering our own lives totally to a life of service, to God. Then, and only then, can we fulfill our responsibility in being born on this planet. Only then can we in Truth say, "I am."

The sacred name of God lies between the words "I" and "am." When you say "I," it is already gone because God never manifests Himself twice in one moment and "am" is in the future. Between "I" and "am" is the name of God. When we are finally abandoned to the one Will, there is only the Truth, and as Mr. Gurdjieff said, "Life is real only when I AM."

There is a patron behind my words — Mevlana, which means "Master" or "My Master." When I say, "Mevlana Jelaluddin Rumi," I talk about a link between this human being, in his relative existence state, and this human being's yearning — towards complete union with God. Mevlana, who reached Union seven hundred years ago, has become for me at last... a link.

This great Persian Sufi of the twelfth century once said these words. I have them written above my desk and I read them many times a day.

Reason is powerless in the expression of Love.

Love alone is capable of revealing the truth of Love and being a Lover.

The way of our prophets is the way of Truth.

If you want to live, die in Love.

Die in Love if you want to remain alive.

— Mevlana Jelaluddin Rumi

THE PATH OF AFFIRMATION

Reshad Feild

There is change, and there is the apparency of change. If we make our commitment to the Work, which is sometimes called the "spirit of God," we commit ourselves to change. We commit ourselves, first of all, to allow ourselves to be changed, and then to becoming an agent for real change to take place in the world around us — in our family, our friends, in society, and in the world as a whole. It is no good pretending to have committed ourselves to the Work if we are not prepared to accept change, and all that it brings with it. It is not useful to put one foot on the path and leave another on the old road. It is not useful, and it can also be dangerous, for real change may then come about before we are prepared for all this entails.

So when we commit ourselves to the Work, we commit ourselves, once and for all, to change. There is no way out. There is no back door through which we can escape. We have made our commitment outside time, and thus have set out on what is called the "Path of Service." We have truly become channels for necessary change — but change when the time is right, when everything is properly prepared.

This principle is illustrated in nature. Without the cycles of change, the planet itself could

not live and give us life. It is through change
that life on earth exists at all. Each season gives
way to another season. It does not fight the
necessity of change, but just gives way, bows to
the next stage — welcomes it home. Spring
gives way to summer, summer to autumn, autumn to winter. And as the cycle goes on and
on, year after year, generation after generation,
the seasons offer us again and again the possibility of learning what is necessary.

Let us look at it this way. One year we plant
potatoes, and the next year, during the same
season, we plant corn on the same land. Each
crop brings about a different set of circumstances, yet each one follows the natural flow of
the seasons. If potatoes were planted in the
same field during the same season each year,
then slowly the soil would be depleted, the
potato crop would fail, and there would be
wastage. Crop rotation provides new food for
the soil, and new types of harvest for those who
sow; thus within the laws governing the cycles
of life we see the apparency of change. One year
we plant this crop, and another year we plant
that. The situation seems to be different, yet it
is only following the laws that govern the seasons of the year. The laws governing the seasons remain the same; the differences that we
see are merely different manifestations of the
same principle.

When Mr. Gurdjieff said "Life is real only
when I AM," he left it to his readers to interpret
this statement on the level from which each
person was working — that level being depen-

dent on the amount of work the individual had done on him or herself. Now perhaps we can look at the meaning behind these words so that the understanding of how change comes about can be more real for us.

"The One divides in order to unite." This concept is familiar from many traditions; what we wish to look at here is just how the One does divide. The cause of creation is Love. God is Love. There is a saying in the Hadith of the Prophet Mohammed (peace and blessings be upon him), "I was a hidden treasure and I loved to be known; so I created the world that I might be known." God divides Himself that He may be known.

The question that we are asking is, how does this come about? It is essentially very simple; in fact, it is simplicity itself! For if we follow the *via negativa*, the way that is based upon negation of the illusion and negation of that which creates the illusion (i.e., the false "I" that feels that it is separate from the unity of all life), then we understand this process as creating a sense of separation of the individual from his or her Creator. Paradoxically, in the path of negation you affirm separation by assuming, in the first place, that there is something to negate; but in Reality, separation must always be an illusion, for there is only One Absolute Being.

He said, "I was a hidden treasure, and I loved to be known." How is it possible for anything to be known, and for that knowledge to be confirmed, if there is not the illusion of separateness? If there were no mirror, then how would we be able to know what we looked like? If there was not the exterior world, the outward form, would there be any chance of knowing the hidden "withinness" of things? In this world it is necessary that there be a vehicle through which there may be knowledge; thus a world of apparent duality is formed.

The apparency of separation, of duality, is necessary for the creative process to unfold; so although the way of negation, aimed at bringing us to a desireless state is a very real way, it is only one half of the picture. The way of the Work in the West is the way of affirmation, but this is made possible only through the way of negation that has gone before. First comes the way of negation, and then comes the way of affirmation. First comes the realization of who and what we are through the discovery that all that we thought we were is illusion — thought being a process that has already past, already gone — and then comes the affirmation of what we really are and thus the beginning of the next stage of the Work.

In the Work we come to know that it is through affirmation, made possible only by negation, that real change can come about. The moment that real change does occur, we are subjected to a totally new set of laws. We have free choice. We can revert to the old set of laws which brought us to the point of negation — think, for example of all that has led you to read what is being said here — or we can make ourselves ready to understand another set of laws that are available to us through committing ourselves to saying "I am." "Life is real only when I AM." Life is made real only when we come to affirm the presence of God by saying "I am!" — not stating that there is separation, but affirming the whole creative process by stating the very word that brings that process into manifestation! "I AM" — "I am" because I know that I am one with God. "I am" because I know that He needs me to affirm Him by saying "I." Through that affirmation He divides Himself in order to unite, a mirror is made, comparison takes place, need is created, desire is born in man, and so we see the ongoing process of evolution.

If we enter the path, and are accepted as workers in this process that we call life, then it is necessary that we know about the different laws to which we are subjected. If we are merely living in the world, being processed by the world, seeking out an existence in the world, then we can quite easily define the laws that control and govern our lives. We might, for example, look at the different laws of the country in which we live, or the laws of the society, or the rules within the family. We could realize that we are subjected to the gravitational pull of the moon, and, if we are interested, we could see how our birth, and (potentially) all that comes after our birth in this world has some dependence on the movements of the planets. Everywhere we look, we will be able to find these laws, and it is even possible to study them and, through the knowledge of them, to live a relatively balanced life. Through following the laws of the family, the society in which we live and work, the country we have chosen to make our home, we can find the most harmonious way of living in that society.

But supposing we enter the Path of Service? Supposing we come upon the Work, which is involved with bringing about real change? What then? When we enter this path we actually put ourselves in touch with an entirely different set of laws, and we would be foolish if we did not study them, and work with them for our own harmony and the harmony of those around us.

Once we truly want to understand what the Work is about, we can no longer revert to the old way of life. There is no point in following the laws of the country we have just left and trying to impose them on the country to which we have gone. There are different circumstances here, and different considerations based upon different needs. Those who already live in this new country know more about what is needed and they do not wish to see us try to impose the old laws into their world. There is no point in this, and no benefit. Nothing real can come out of this sort of action. Rather we make our journey to this new land, and then, in humility, we ask of those who already live in that place what rules they have found to help fulfill the natural order of life. Only if we ask can we possibly learn what is required of us and thus find out how we can be of service.

The average man, subject to the laws that govern the life we experience in this world, is subject only to the laws that arise out of "want" and "desire" — wanting something for "me," the desire to do this or that which is directly related to the word "me". Yet it is not the "I" that knows the purpose of that affirmation, but it is the "I" that feels itself separate from everything else, and which continues a process of the apparency of change. It is not the "I" that knows that through affirmation it is participating in the evolutionary process itself.

For those who enter upon the Path of Service there are two sets of laws. There are laws based upon want and desire, but now we are subject also to laws based upon need. This is what we are asked to consider — the meaning of the word "need," and all that it implies.

Through negation we discover what we, as individuals, do not need. We find out that the things we thought we needed were not truly necessary. We might have wanted them; we might still want them, but we do not need them any more.

So through the *via negativa*, it is discovered that want and need are two entirely different concepts. Want and desire arise each moment of our lives in the relative world, but real need is God's need. It is the need for us to turn to Him alone and thus to be able to know what needs to be done in order to fulfill God's plan for this world. Need is based upon time — not the time we create from our own desires, but from the natural flow of life itself. The need is established before time as we experience it.

Night and day, sun and moon, the turn of the seasons are the first stages of the unfoldment of a principle that existed before time. After these stages, a series of laws appears that governs the real world — first the law of three forces, and then the law of seven forces, or the octave of life. The planet turns on its axis while orbiting the sun, creating the seasons; and then, awakened man, conscious man, becomes the agent to bring these next two great laws into manifestation.

God is Love and Love becomes relative only when we desire, when we want, and when we apply the word "I" to life. The false "I" is made of the substance created out of desire, and yet if there were no desire then the Love of God could not unfold itself into the relative world. This is perhaps one of the greatest paradoxes for the aspirant on the path. We are asked to give up our desire and to come to understand the real world, and yet God needs for us to say "I" if there is to be any change, any on-going process in our world. God needs man to say "I," having affirmed his unity with God in saying "I am" so that life has, at last, become real for him.

Desire is relative; Love is absolute. The former without the latter is impossible; and yet without our desire, our yearning, Love cannot break out of Unity and bring about the miracle of diversity. God needs for us to want to know Him and thus to be awake to the laws that govern real change within the cycles set before time.

We have free choice. We can remain in the tight knot of *samsara*, governed by the old laws based upon want and desire, or we can begin to learn from those who have already seen into the real world and know the laws that are necessary for a new order to come on Earth. The East has traditionally followed the way of negation. Now the West, through all that has gone before, is asked to follow the path of affirmation in the knowledge of the Unity of God, knowing that in saying "I am" life becomes real for the first time, and thus we begin to fulfill our destiny in being born man and woman.

THE WALLS THAT DIVIDE US

Reshad Feild

In several of my books I have mentioned "the three walls" that divide us — walls that divide us from one another and from the realization of Unity for which we yearn. It is this yearning which brought us to study and work together in the first place. These are the walls of *envy, resentment* and *pride*.

When I was first told of these walls, it all seemed too easy, and since it was necessary to translate what I was being told from Turkish into English, I felt that there must have been some mistake. What arrogance! It is the very simplest of concepts that are often the most difficult to face. It is when everything is very simple that the mirror is almost too close for comfort.

Let us look at these three words for a moment. We often use the word *resentment* in our daily lives. We resent this or that happening to us, and we often express our resentment in strong words. We resent what we see happening in the world as well. We ask questions based on resentment — questions such as "Why do the children have to suffer?" or "Why is there still starvation in the Sudan?" or "Surely the massacre in Peking was horrible; these things need to be changed," etc. We also spend a lot of time talking about ecology, pollution, future hopes and aspirations. But I wonder, if we were to look inside ourselves first, we would see that what we are actually reacting to is that wall of resentment that divides us. Can we see clearly when clouds of resentment, built up, perhaps over several generations, are standing between us and the Divine Light? Can we see that a Light is necessary to cut through the clouds and see the real meaning and purpose behind the apparency of things in this phenomenal world? These are vast questions that can only be answered in the innermost honesty of the heart.

To understand the meaning of this we need to look at the subject of change. If we resent something, it is usually because we are either incapable of changing something to be the way that we want it to be, or else something has already changed, dramatically affecting our lives. We have been swept into change through circumstances apparently outside our control. We do not like it; it does not suit our concepts of how things should be. Time has overtaken us and we were taken unawares. We may even start blaming others for this, and get our friends to agree with us, thus giving weight to our argument, and before long we are swept away from the Straight Way that we set out to follow when we began our journey on the Path of Return. We are blinded and even lost.

We are human beings. We are mortals, and therefore imperfect. Since this phenomenal world is merely a world of appearances, nothing in it can be absolutely perfect, because everything is in a state of change. Even a mountain is slowly changing, as is a glacier which moves imperceptibly forwards and downwards. Everything is in a state of change; nothing remains static. Yet, so often we attempt to keep things as they are (as we want them to be) so that we can avoid the fear that arises when change is inevitable.

It reminds me of the man in a punt on the river. It is a lovely summer's day. A beautiful woman lies in the boat, the picnic hamper awaits the time for lunch. The champagne is cold, the lady's dress is enchanting. The sun is warm and birds are singing. The man hums to himself, punting along the river, first his pole flung high into the air and then plunged down into the water to hit the bottom of the river, and so propel the boat, himself, and his lady onwards to their destination. The air quivers with expectation.

Then the inevitable happens. The man, taking a particularly powerful stroke with his pole, gets the pole firmly stuck in the bottom of the river. The mud is heavy and the pole sticks fast. The river, on the other hand, moves onwards (as rivers always do). And now, the only steering that the boat has is with the punt-pole which is now stuck in the bottom of the river. The man struggles desperately, trying to pull up the pole. The boat swerves from side to side; the lady shouts in dismay. We now see a picture of the man holding onto the very end of the pole, lying almost horizontally with the water but still stuck in the mud behind the boat. The river is too strong. Fearfully he hangs on for one last effort. The boat is in the fast water, the lady in distress, and the man, still hanging onto the pole, falls into the water as the boat moves on down the river.

There are things in the outer world that we cannot change, however much we would like them to be different. There is Destiny and there is Fate, and it would be incorrect not to try to change what we consider to be wrong if we can actually do something about any given situation.

It is important that we look at our own condition at the time we want to take action. Do we feel some sort of resentment? If so, it is much better to wait until that moment has passed and we can see a little more clearly. By acting too hastily, and in resentment, we can delay the gentle, more subtle change that might have been going on for a long time, and thus precipitate dramatic and even violent upsets to bring about the necessary change.

We all know that there is a definite feeling connected with resentment. We are all uniquely different and therefore it would be foolish to try to make a general statement as to what this sensation might be. However, we will usually feel the sensation in the area of our solar plexus or even lower down. There is often that "sinking feeling" when we know we have made a mistake. The first sensation can then sink even lower, bringing us from fear, into grief, and then into apathy where there is an inability to care sufficiently to be able to bring us back up the scale into balance.

We must build what is sometimes called the "observer" into our lives. We need to learn to recognize how, and later why, we react to a given situation. Are we reacting out of resentment? It is not such a difficult task, but it takes constant effort in awareness and conscious breathing in order to be sufficiently awake. Then, supposing we recognize that we are about to act with resentment as our motivator, we can wait and instead look carefully and honestly at ourselves. Thus, little by little, we are breaking down one of the walls that divide us. It is surely recognition that is the first step.

If the first step is recognizing that we are acting in resentment, then the second step is to ask ourselves just what this resentment actually is. We will soon realize that it is involved with change, and therefore the nature of time. The secret of time lies in the moisture that is carried on the breath. If water is a conductor of electricity, and if a thought-form can be seen to be an electrical impulse, then it is not difficult to see that there is a direct connection between thought and time, whether moving in from the past or out toward the future. Why is it more difficult to breathe out than to breathe in? Could it be that if we really did breathe out correctly, we would be truly letting go of what is not necessary from the past so that the future could bring us into the world of possibilities? Here is a good challenge!

Now let us look at the second wall which is the wall of envy. Perhaps this is not so difficult to understand as the first one. After all, we know that it is often envy that would make us break one of the great Commandments. It is said, "Thou shalt not steal" and of course there are many levels concerned with this law. There is the obvious breaking of the law when we take someone else's property which we covet, but then there are more subtle ways of looking at this law. How often, for example, do we unwittingly steal energy from another? That is worth considering. Certainly it is something to be watched very carefully. If we do such a thing, it is coming from a rebound off the wall of envy. Someone "out there" has a certain sort of energy that we want. We feel that we do not have it, that we deserve it, and wonder why one person should have so much and we so little. Therefore we try to take some of that energy from the other person, and it most likely gives us indigestion because we don't yet know how to deal with it.

Envy is just another description of the results of our sense of separation, and yet, if we did not feel separate we would not want to return to Unity. That is the Divine Comedy, the riddle and game that is with us all the time. There is no point resenting it and there is no point in being envious of someone else who can see the game clearer than we can. It is perfectly possible for everyone to see the game and eventually find their own part to play in it, if we understand its purpose and work hard to be awake.

Lastly we come to the wall of pride. Perhaps this is the most difficult one of all to find and understand. Like the other walls, it may make life very upsetting and sometimes unbearable, but it is given to us for a purpose. Each time one of the stones in the wall is removed there is a little more light, but imagine what would happen if all the stones were removed at once? Surely the light would be too much to bear. So we move forward carefully, step by step, calling to the One Guide to keep us on the Straight Way, and perhaps, with a little help from our friends, we remove the stones one by one. With perseverance we continue, and with faith and trust we take down the stones of resentment, envy, and pride and transform them into new and beautiful buildings for our children and our children's children.

Whenever we feel "special," it is pride that is our motivator. Oh, but pride is so subtle! How often do we suffer from false humility, thinking or feeling that we are truly humble and very much on the path of service? So "we" are on the path of service and "others" are not. More separation. Perhaps we feel inadequate and even useless at times. Tut! Tut! There is always something that we can do, whether visibly or invisibly, known or unknown to our friends and acquaintances. We are meant to be creative human beings. We cease to be creative when we feel special, for then that great big, thick wall of pride even blots out the sun and thus there is no growth within us. Everything is reaching towards the light, and just as the trees and the beautiful flowers seek out the light, so does Beauty herself seek out the light within us. As long as Beauty is covered by these walls, She cannot be one with the Light who created Her in the first place.

In considering pride, we can follow the same advice as with the wall of resentment, by building in the Observer and seeing how we act and react. Do we react from pride or don't we? Do we feel special and separate or can we understand the Mercy and Compassion of God and so begin again fresh with each moment?

Perhaps some of you are feeling that this is all too simple. There must be more to do than this. Of course there is endless work to be done on ourselves and discourses that can be written about the subject. But, when you can watch and observe and be honest about the sense of separation that we all feel, you will come closer to the walls. And then, gently, you can reach out to each stone and brick that needs to be removed. You can go hand in hand together in the One Brotherhood of Man in the Fatherhood of God and help one another. It is those stones and bricks that can be washed and transformed in love to help build the "platform" for the Second Cycle of Mankind.

CLEANLINESS

Reshad Feild

Cleanliness has to be both personal, and impersonal. Personal cleanliness is, relatively speaking, obvious. If we are dirty, we cannot expect others to get too close to us. If we are dirty, we attract dirt, for that is the law of the game.

In my tradition, as in any other living tradition, ablutions are of extreme importance. We wash that we can pray. We wash that we can truly make love. We wash that we can be clear channels to serve God. We cannot expect God to wash us, for he gives us the instruments that we wash ourselves!

It is the same in a sacred space or in any house given to God. As custodians of such a house, we have the privilege to serve the house and all those who enter its gates. We yearn to serve, and thus we find joy in keeping the house clean and full of His light, which cannot shine if dirt exists. After all, even a house plant is partially veiled if the leaves are covered in dust.

A house given to God is a house that is open to the guest, and in Reality there is only One Guest. Would the Guest wish to enter a place that is not clean? Would He wish to sleep on a bed that was not spotless? Would He wish to eat from a kitchen that did not sing with the Divine Light?

It is not difficult to understand the answer if we are truly honest with ourselves. After all, would we, as guests, wish to enter our friend's house, only to find that there was no clean towel with which to wash, no soap in the basin, no clean bath to wash in, in order to be able to be good guests?

There are other, more esoteric reasons for cleanliness. Dirt attracts psychic dirt, and psychic dirt attracts resentment. If we are in a state of resentment, no longer wishing to serve our fellow human being, who surely can be the manifestation of the One Guest, then we will not be of Service. Perhaps we will produce food that is not to our guest's liking, or we will forget that our guest might like some fresh flowers in his or her room, a smiling face to welcome him, and a loving heart to receive him.

If a church, or ashram, or tekke, or even a home is working correctly, then by the very act of entering the building, there is the possibility of change within us. Ironically, if a holy man comes into the space, there is always more cleaning that is necessary, for by his very presence alone, man can be transformed. Thus there is a subconscious letting-go of our problems, our resentment, envy, or pride — whatever, and it has to go somewhere. It does not fly off into the ether somewhere. It has to be transformed, "eaten" — brought back into the light.

It would be hard, even for the greatest Guru, or Swami, or Shaykh, to help facilitate this if he were sitting in a bed of stale nettles!

Please let your house be a true house of God, always ready to receive the Guest. Let us give up our preconceived ideas of what this could mean by serving first of all, the functional level. Then, *Insh'Allah*, God willing, the Guest will come, and through our own outer and inner cleanliness, we will be able to see Him.

BREATH, The Secret of Life

Reshad Feild

> *All is contained in the Divine Breath*
> *Like the day in the morning's dawn.*
> *-Ibn al-'Arabi*

There was a small group of people living in a community in New England who built a 34-foot aeolian harp and placed it on top of a mountain. As you probably know, the original aeolian harp, tuned in a special manner, was made to be played by the wind. These young people made this unusual experiment together and made a recording of the extraordinarily beautiful music of the wind blowing through the harp. The recordings, made in spring, summer, autumn and winter, had a profound effect on me when I first heard them.

The first step towards a deep understanding of breath is to learn how to breathe in a way that our subtle bodies are finely tuned in the same way that the harp was tuned to respond to the wind. It is so easy to take breathing for granted and forget that it is almost an obligation in our lives to learn how to breathe consciously. However, if we live life passionately and really love being here, we will come to want to explore the depths of this great miracle called breath.

When the wind changes we know that something different will happen in our world. There is the wind of change blowing over the face of the earth even now. Where and how does the wind start? Scientists can tell us many technical things about this, but there are other, more profound explanations that can be discovered from inner work.

We too can be played by the wind, and what we speak will be the sound of the moment, bringing with the word, the possibility of real change rather than the apparency of change. We all know this somewhere deep within ourselves, and although God gives us everything, it is up to us to be so finely tuned that the music that is played is of Truth itself. Did not Mevlana Jelaluddin Rumi say, "We are the flute, but the music is Thine."

Breath is the secret of life, for without breath there is nothing. With correct breathing it is possible to choose the way you wish to travel. Think of the wind — it blows and carries with it whatever is light enough to be lifted from the earth. It carries the scent of flowers, it carries the leaves as they fall from the trees, and it carries the seeds from the plants to the place where they may take root. There is a great message here! We come into this world on the breath and we go out of this world on the breath. The average man, living his life in a mechanical way, forgets all about breathing until the moment of his death when he struggles to draw air into his lungs, clutching to the last remnants of what he has known as life in this world.

The practice of breath can be done every day, every moment, for the rest of your life. It seems easy, but as each moment is different, at times you may find it impossible to concentrate. But little by little you will come to understand the importance of what I am telling you.

First, you must learn how to purify the subtle bodies by surrendering the concept of the physical body so that you may come upon that invisible matrix from which the body is continuously being formed. If you learn how to purify yourself, you will be able to see more clearly as the thought forms and projections that obstruct clear sight and inner hearing begin to dissolve. After all, thought is the only thing that divides us.

First make sure that your back is straight, and then simply watch the rise and fall of the breath. To be able to do this takes much practice, and few people are prepared to make the necessary effort. When you can just watch the breath you will begin to realize that we are tyrannized by thoughts that move us this way and that, almost constantly; and although we do not like to face the truth, it becomes clear to us that we have little of permanence. But you are not your thoughts, any more than you are your emotions or your body. If you are not your thoughts, and yet you find it so difficult to just watch the breath and not be moved by these thoughts, then is there not something wrong?

Until you have a permanent "I" you will always be in danger of being led astray. When you learn to breathe in awareness, there is a chance to come upon this inner being that is your real self.

There are three aspects of breath. The science of breathing is the study of a lifetime, but these three aspects, if considered carefully and put into practice, can help change the course of your life. They are the rhythm of the breath, the quality of the breath, and the positioning of the breath.

Much has been written recently in the West about the rhythm of the breath, called *pranayama* in India, but people do not realize that the different kinds of rhythms taught by different schools and teachers are meant to produce different results. If you want to drive a car very fast up a hill, the engine takes on quite a different rhythm than when it is coasting gently down the hill. The speed of the car may be the same, but the rhythm of the engine is quite different. It is the same in the science of breath — the understanding of rhythm is vital.

The rhythm I am going to teach you is sometimes called the "mother's breath." People do not realize that something is being "born" out of every moment, and that if we could find the rhythm that is most natural and most in harmony with the universal laws governing our existence, we would be contributing to the work of bringing about peace on this planet.

Make sure your spine is straight, so that the vital fluids can pass easily up and down. Now, inhale to a count of seven, pause for one, and breathe out for a count of seven. Before breathing in to start the second cycle, pause once more on the out breath for a count of one. This is a very simple rhythmic count of 7-1-7-1-7. If you work hard the timing will soon become automatic.

Let go of all concepts. Surrender to the rhythm that flows and pulsates throughout all life. This rhythm is called the law of seven, and by following it you establish yourself as part of the harmonious principle of life which wishes only to conceive perfection from within itself. The "mother's breath" helps us to see the infinite possibility lying in the here and now, like the physical womb.

This rhythm of the breathing helps us to see that the present moment pulsates, expanding and contracting, coming into existence and passing out of it again instantaneously. Everything is born from this rhythmic pulsation of "the womb of the moment." This rhythm also produces the waves of vibration that make up the subtle or formative worlds interpenetrating the grosser physical substance. It's all just a question of different rates of vibration: The slower the rate, the denser the material; the higher the rate of vibration, the more refined and less stable the substance. And the rate of pulsation is the same as the rhythm of the breath, 7-1-7.

The next stage is concerned with the quality of the air you breathe. Just as the wind carries on its wings whatever is light enough to be lifted from the earth, there are many qualities that can be carried on the breath if we understand rhythm, and if we are able to concentrate correctly. For example, you could choose one color out of the whole spectrum and breathe it into your body, infusing each cell. This practice is useful in certain types of healing. You can breathe in a strong vibration, similar to the low notes of the piano, or you can choose to breathe in the finest vibration imaginable which, in this world, would be beyond the range of sound. You can choose anything! You could breathe in the elements of fire, earth, air or water. You could breathe in the essence of a particular flower or herb. The science of breath is a vast subject, known only to a few in the past, but now it is time for the world to begin to understand.

The third aspect I wish to touch on is the placing of breath. Just as the wind carries the seed from one place to another, so the breath can carry intention from one area of the body to another for special purposes. Through correct placing of the breath we can learn to bring the body into balance. We can begin to learn the art of transmutation, the art of the alchemists. We can begin to fulfill our responsibility in being conscious human beings devoted to a life of service on earth.

TIME & PERSEVERANCE

Reshad Feild

It is said in the *I Ching*, the Chinese book of divination, "Perseverance furthers," and although this is an obvious statement, it would be worthwhile to go a little deeper into its inner meaning.

The moment we use the word *perseverance* it is inevitable that we bring in the subject of time. So often we merely presume time; we accept it in its inevitability. We know a little about it, and yet, possibly through fear of life itself, we seldom probe deeply into its inner meaning. If we persevere on the Road of Truth, then we are passing *through* time as we normally know it. We are parting the waves of time with the sword of Truth, to finally be able to see beyond the confines of time into other worlds which come under different laws than the ones we normally experience in our very primitive state. We can see that we live mostly dependent on animal instinct, behaving like sleepwalkers in a dream-state. Luckily, there are other ways of living. There are immense possibilities open to us as we begin to wake up to the "Real World."

To persevere, it is necessary that we set goals for ourselves and persist in our desire to fulfill these goals. This may sound selfish, but since we are all so vitally interconnected it is not entirely selfish. If we truly come to find ourselves, then there is a liquid gold that passes out through the invisible network of which we are all a part. Our own perseverance and the sacrifices that we have to make on the pathway are distilled and form this liquid gold, which eases the way for the Message to be heard. That is why our Path is called "The Way of Love, Compassion, and Service."

A goal also requires conscious use of time. It is not good enough to just vaguely make a goal without knowing the correct decision-making process and understanding the nature of time itself. A goal that is limited by the sort of time we normally experience may do some good but it cannot produce the alchemical process that is necessary in the transformation of the individual and even the planet itself.

So now let us look at time as we normally experience it. The first aspect is what I call "natural time." This is the time in which we experience life. There is conception, there is birth, there is our life-span and then there is something that is known as death. It is an endless circle of patterns repeating themselves. It is the knot of *samsara*, the patterns merely repeating themselves in slightly different ways in order to suit the moment and form a mirror into which we may even see the illusion of it all, and thus start to break free from this prison.

Other effects of time come into play on this theatrical stage we call life. For example, we have the seasons — spring, summer, autumn, and winter, all of which have some effect on the timing of our lives. After all, what we plant in one season we harvest in another. Even the geographical position in which we live has its own effect since what is planted in one season and in one place on the planet is planted at exactly the opposite time on the other side of the planet. We go shopping in Zurich and buy papayas that were planted in Hawaii while we were asleep in the middle of winter! It is an amazing life, to be sure, and yet we so often merely presume it. We just take it for granted.

In our time we are also directly influenced by the movement of the planets and the stars in the heavens. Each planet, as we know, has its own time-cycle in its journey around the sun. There is indeed something in us which is influenced in the time process that is set up by the movement of the planets. Thus, astrologers are given to us and predictions of all sorts take place. In many cases there is much truth in them, that is, until we can break from the tyranny of time, and thus, even break the influence of our astrological charts. It *is* possible. We are told this in the sacred documents. However, it would be a stupidly ambitious task to try to break our astrological clock until the time was exactly and precisely correct and we were prepared to ride that magic carpet through the barriers of time itself.

Supposing we could actually create time ourselves? I mean create time consciously, not limited by identification with our lower emotions. To do so, it is necessary to go way beyond the illusion that time just moves from left to right, from the "beginning" to the "end." That is a limitation, as though we are threaded, like beads on an eternal necklace hanging around our necks, strangling us, even taking away the breath of life that we are given. Eventually we are snuffed out like candles on a yearly birthday cake. It is not a very happy proposition!

In one sense, time does move from left to right as we have described, but time is also coming *into* the present moment. *All transformation takes place in the present moment* — both the redemption of past mistakes (stemming from lack of knowledge in the first place) and the redemption of those thought-forms that have been projected into the future from the past, (producing so much unhappiness down the ages, the unhappiness created by the expectation of our parents and forebears who have projected their own wishes and their own failures upon the children). "Don't worry son," says the father on his death-bed, "I know you can make it. You can take over what I have left."

Time-past, time-present, and time-future can be understood through the analogy of two trains, one moving from left to right, from the past into the future, and one waiting in the future to be brought into the present moment. When the time is right and we are ready, we can call the engine driver of the future coming in and beckon him to come on home to meet the train of the past in the present moment, so that, with one cry of recognition, there is completion at last. All that is seen to have been is, and will be, forever in the present moment.

For this to be understood it is essential that we persevere in our questions, in our yearning from the heart, and in our search for Truth. Perseverance requires courage on all levels. It requires compassion and endless patience. "The last shall be first and the first shall be last," it is said in the Bible, and in the Sufi tradition the first Name of God, "Compassion," has the same number as the last of His Most Holy Names, "Patience."

In our work we are asked to remember, with each moment of our lives, that we are all interconnected. "You cannot pick a flower without the troubling of a star," and so, since in reality everything is in the present moment, our efforts can even break the genetic patterns of the past, so that our children and our children's children no longer have to repeat our own patterns and those of our parents and ancestors, but rather, can walk more freely on this earth.

We do not have to look far to understand these things. That which is nearest to us is where we'll find the key to unlock Pandora's box. Since God made man and woman in His image, it is in our neighbor that we can find at least half the answer, for he is the mirror of ourselves. Hazrat Inayat Khan said, "If only you explore him, there is a lot in man." It is also stated in the two great commandments, "Love the Lord thy God," and "Love thy neighbor as thyself."

I offer these seed thoughts as a challenge to

your own logical thinking mechanism. Logical thinking goes from one concept to another, and only works in the train going from left to right. It is unable to step forward to ring the bell for the train to come in from the apparently unknowable future, like the prodigal son returning to the arms of his father. "A Sufi is the son of the moment" — the present moment. As in the parable in the Gospel of Luke, logical thinking man stays at home and apparently keeps out of trouble. Prodigal son goes out into the future and returns, bringing with him all the hope for the future into the present moment. The father embraces him and there is great rejoicing. It is then that logical thinking man realizes that he has missed out all the time.

Take a big step. "The first step starts a journey of a thousand miles," (American Indian saying). Today is the only time that we can have dominion over ourselves. This is the only day that we can bask in the sun of realization. We have this day. We have this hour. All is in the one eternal moment out of which universes are born, and within which we can return to our Source.

Perseverance furthers! May the two engine drivers hold hands on the station of peace in our own hearts at last.

Part Two

THE WAY TO PRAY

Reshad Feild

Many people ask me, "How does one pray?" So, I felt that it was necessary to attempt to write something about the subject. But it is a hard task, indeed, and please remember that anything I say can only be written from a very personal standpoint. Not following any set form or belief system and not being a scholar, it would be foolhardy to attempt to give some sort of comparative religion class on the subject. After all, if you study the life of the Christian mystic, Julian of Norwich, the results of her prayerfulness brought her near death. But that was what she wanted. She wanted to walk the road of the Cross and therefore that was the way she experienced the Passion. Also, please do remember that people like Julian lived in another epoch, another era. They were ascetic celibates and so it's a very different matter from the sort of lives we lead today.

For the moment, please, allow me to generalize somewhat. In the Hindu tradition, for example, there is much prayerfulness. In as far as the Western mind is concerned, there is very much superstition tied up with all the different deities, the bells, the gongs, and the incense. It is hard to reconcile from our Western point of view the self-negation and suffering that some of the ascetics in India put themselves through.

For me, it is equally hard to reconcile the self-imposed suffering of the Catholic flagellants. When I was in Greece, I personally witnessed the main street in Corfu virtually dripping with blood as the flagellants beat themselves along the road while a group of people carried the remains of the patron saint in an enormous casket. I have witnessed scenes in India and in the East which, in the name of religion or spirituality, would make one's hair stand on end. And yet, religion comes from the word *religiare* which means "return to God through law," and therefore, ultimately, through God. I wonder what on Earth He would think about it all? After all, He had to create the world that He might be known. Well, that's a pretty funny way to do it. I have often talked about freedom and asked people to question the meaning of the word. After all, there is freedom for, freedom from, and freedom in. For example, there is freedom in true knowledge since it is knowledge that anchors love.

Is it not similar in prayer? There is prayer to God or to the gods. There is prayer to the Lord in supplication, the Lord seen here as the mediator between man and his creator. And there is prayer in God, in the realization of His Unity. Ultimately, it could be said that God prays Himself in us as His witnesses. And so, we are both the results of His prayer and the sounding box for His creation, calling out the message of freedom to the world.

You see, it is a vast subject. Again I say that it is very personal for all of us. For those people who have never been brought up in a tradition of prayer, it is a question of where and how to start. For me, alone in my room in a prayerful attitude, I just see myself as incapable of doing anything without God, without Allah. Since indeed, He is the only Provider, the only Guide, the only safe refuge, and so on. So I turn to God. There is nothing else better to do. Yet at the same time, we must not fall into further and further separation by seeing Him "out there," as it were.

And yet, we're also told that "all is within." And to this I reply with a question: "Within what?" When there is no within or without, then our prayers are answered, for surely it is Union with the One Source of all Life, the Divine, whatever words you want, that is the yearning of the soul.

I will give you a little story to illustrate what the Christians call "the fear of God."

Recently I was not well, and was finally forced to go to a doctor. The day before I went to the doctor, I'd been in bed, unable to face the situation and in great pain. However, the next day, I managed to get out of bed and face going to the doctor. When I arrived at the doctor's office, the pain had virtually all gone. Maybe the doctor is God.

When we can face what we have to face, the pain of living goes. Can you see what I'm getting at? In Zen Buddhism it's said, "If you meet Buddha on the street, kill him!" The meaning is obvious. The Buddha in his time represented what was necessary for God's sake in the world. He sat under the banyan tree to seek out enlightenment and thus Buddhism was formed. Like all things, Buddhism split first into two, Theravada and then Mahayana Buddhism, and then onwards into many different sects.

> *The One creates the two, the two the three and the three the ten thousand things.*
>
> — *the Tao Teh Ching*

I've often said, sometimes causing much trouble, that the more you pray to God, the less of God there is. Or is it, the less of one's *nafs*, or false ego, there is? Or is it, just as we realize we are both hopeless and helpless, the less separation there is?

Now, is there a need to pray? Good question. The answer can only be realized through the heart. For me, I know that I can do nothing without accepting the completion of the line of the prophets, the Prophet Mohammed, peace and blessings upon him and his family, as well as the entire line of the prophets, including Adam, Abraham, and the Seal of Sanctity as realized in Jesus Christ. And I pray to God in gratefulness for His nearest servants throughout time.

That does not mean to say that it's not just as beneficial for orthodox Christian people to pray to their Lord acting as their mediator, for that is their way. Even the most innocent child praying to an unknown God helps prayers be answered for us all. We can pray now, and time is either past, present, or future, but in one time or another, our prayers are answered. Maybe my Mother's prayers are answered in my prayers for the world. Maybe your Father's prayers, and your Mother's prayers, and your ancestors' prayers are answered in your prayer for the world in the present moment.

Yes, I would say it is a good thing to pray. Let us remember, however, that to "Let His will be done" is not just the profession of our own thoughts and aspirations. Hazrat Inayat Khan said, "Let Thy wish become my desire." It is the same, surely, as the words that Jesus Christ asked us to say when he said, "Let Thy Will be done on Earth as it is in Heaven."

The Jewish tradition teaches us to pray to the One, and yet, strangely and beautifully enough, the greatest Jew who ever lived taught us to say, "Our Father who art in Heaven." Jesus did not make the prayer just for some of the world. He gave it to everyone. The same thing applies exactly and precisely with the Islamic prayer, the Fatiha. I was able through music, harmonics and sound to bring together the Lord's Prayer and the Fatiha because I understood the mystical marriage of Christianity and Islam.

And so, my friends, it is for you to find out what prayer is. It is the humility of a child. It is the beauty of Being. And it is the love of being alive.

Mevlana Jelaluddin Rumi said, "Many things will happen, ask God to inform you." So ask God how to pray with all the sincerity, honesty, humility, and passion you have within you. Just ask how He wants you to pray. And I'm sure that one day your prayer, which will be His prayer, will be answered.

LORD'S PRAYER

Traditional

Our Father Who art in Heaven,
Hallowed be thy Name.

Thy Kingdom come, Thy Will be done, on
earth as it is in Heaven.

Give us this day our daily bread.

And forgive us our trespasses, as we
forgive those that trespass against us.

Lead us not into temptation,
But deliver us from evil.

For Thine is the Kingdom, and the Power,
and the Glory,

Forever and ever.

Amen.

CONTEMPLATION ON THE LORD'S PRAYER

Reshad Feild

The Lord's Prayer can be used as a contemplation by taking each sentence into our meditation, letting it sink into the very center of our being, and praying that we may be granted the understanding that emerges from the soul itself.

"Our Father Who art in Heaven,"

The Father is the Lord, and the secret of Lordship is Thou. Your Lord and my Lord are different, and yet in reality there is only one Lord. "Our Father," the Lord of Lords, is "in Heaven," that is, in a state of perfect order. He contains within himself the whole of the invisible world, in its hierarchical state, each section, each angel and archangel, whatever words we wish to use, perfectly arrayed and aligned in their respective grades.

Heaven descends in one instant onto the earth, to bring about perfect order. This is the act of redemption. Our Father, the Lord of Lords, contains in that heavenly state the perfect order needed to transform earth into Heaven, and Heaven into earth. As above, so below. This transformation leads us to discover that it is this world which is the Resurrection. The Hereafter is right here, now, and the golden key is under our foot.

"Hallowed be thy Name."

It is said that the name of God can never be spoken. People have searched high and low for the Name that will bring about release, or bring about the power which they crave. Yet the name of God cannot be sounded, for it lies between the words "I" and "Am." As soon as you say "I," the moment has already gone, and "Am" is in the future, which does not exist.

God never manifests twice in one moment, thus we are seeking the split second between the bud and the rose, between "I" and "Am." If we come to understand that "Time is the eternal attribute of God," then we can only hallow the name that cannot be spoken.

"Man does not live by bread alone, but by every word that proceedeth out of the mouth of God." Man is the mouth of God. In this realization, we can come to accept the responsibility of being born. This is the responsibility of saying "I am", the words that contain in the unspoken silence, His most Holy Name. "Life is real only when I AM," (Gurdjieff).

"Thy Kingdom come, Thy Will be done, on earth as it is in Heaven."

"Seek ye first the Kingdom of God." The Kingdom is likened unto a mustard seed, the smallest seed that we can imagine. This seed is the center of centers, wherein it is discovered that the center is the periphery and the periphery is nowhere. This center is the point with no dimension, which turns into dimension through Man. It is through the Spirit, through the Christ, that the point with no dimension can be turned into dimension on all the different levels that are necessary to build the new Jerusalem.

"Thy Kingdom come." The Kingdom is the whole invisible space that is the space of God. The Kingdom is the Divine Mother, the matrix of our true self and from which we are born into eternal life. Let us come to recognize the Mother, Mary, so that His Will may be done on earth, the physical counterpart of the Divine Mother, as it is in Heaven. This state of perfect order remains latent, waiting to spiritualize matter, and spread its seed upon the earth.

"Thy Will be done." Will is Spirit. The Work is the Spirit of God. Let us learn to give up our own little wills for the Greater Will, so that the unredeemed chaos will be redeemed to bring about perfect order.

"Thy Will be done on earth as it is in Heaven." O Lord, lead us to remember that it is the Work, Thy Spirit, that comes first, that we may always be of service to Thee.

"Give us this day our daily bread."

"Bread" and "mind" are really the same thing. The stuff of mind, mind-stuff, is unredeemed energy, and redeemed energy is the Spirit. "Give us this day our daily bread." Give us, O Lord, the opportunity to be of service so that the very stuff of the mind may become the substance of the soul. Give us the opportunity to breathe in the unredeemed energy of the world and let it be converted, through us, into Spirit.

"And forgive us our trespasses, as we forgive those that trespass against us."

Forgive us our mistakes. A mistake is any action that can reverse itself. Let us know that we are indeed forgiven instantaneously at the very moment we forgive others. When we have ceased to judge, to blame, we will come to know that there is only one Judge, one Forgiver, one Absolute Being.

Yet God needs man — man being the mouth-piece of His Word. "In the beginning was the Word and the Word was with God." The word proceeds forth from God and goes on its way toward manifestation in the relative world when it is spoken through man.

Teach us that no harm can come to us, for we are nothing, there is only Him. "Father forgive them for they know not what they do." If they knew, they would not speak as they do.

"Lead us not into temptation,"

Let us not be led into the world of attraction. "Falling in love" means coming into Love, coming into Being, and then falling into this world. We cannot come to Love through attraction, the temptation that is with us each moment of our lives. Yet if we come into Love, then we see the whole world as a world of Beauty. The sole purpose of Love is Beauty.

Lead us not, O Father, into forgetfulness of the object of our search. Let us not be led astray by the unleashed forces of attraction. Is not the object of our search Thyself? Is not the cause of all creation Love itself? And, is not Thy yearning greater than ours can ever be for Thee?

"But deliver us from evil."

Good and evil, the polar opposites. May we rise above them to come to know Thee. Deliver us from ignorance, deliver us from sin, and what is sin but lack — lack of knowledge. *La Illaha Il Allah,* "There is no God, but He that is God." Beyond God, beyond all the concepts of God which have their relative opposite, there is Him that makes it all possible. Deliver us from ignorance that we may come upon the Universal Truth beyond all good and evil, right and wrong, recognizing that the One divides in order to unite.

"For Thine is the Kingdom, and the Power, and the Glory,"

"O Thou, the sustainer of our bodies, hearts, and souls, bless all that we receive in thankfulness." All is Thine, and will be returned to Thee, O Lord. The Kingdom, containing within it the Knowledge which is the Divine Power itself, and the Glory which is the realization of our essential unity with Thee. Indeed what I am is the Love, the Lover, and the Beloved, yet all is Thine and I give it back to Thee with every breath of my body.

"Forever and ever."

"As above, so below," at-one-ment, in one moment, in that flash of creation that is now and forevermore.

Amen.

ON PRAYER,
Advice To My Sons
Reshad Feild

If you pray do not pray half-heartedly. Pray with every part of your being. Let your physical body resound to your intention, your feelings and your thoughts. Let prayer manifest in your life's motives and in your aspirational body. Beyond all else, trust that your prayers will be answered as they are needed to be answered.

Prayer is for the very brave. Self-pity, in the apparency of prayer, is for the weak-hearted. Prayer carries the sound of intention, so let your prayer carry the sound of your deepest love, for most surely Love is the cause of life and Love is its own effect.

Understand that prayer is not limited to any religious belief system. It is universal as Love is universal, so part of our life's work is to become so universal in our words, thoughts, feelings and deeds that we become "the sounding box of God."

Beloved Lord Prayer

Reshad Feild

Beloved Lord, Almighty God,

Aside from Whom there is nothing else,

Please help us to love Thee more.

Teach us to realize that the sole purpose of love is beauty.

Bring us to know Thee as Thou art and to find Thee in the one place that is big enough to contain Thee —

The heart of Perfect Man.

Amen.

One Pointed Prayer

"Naked Intent of the Soul"

God, unto whom all hearts are open,

unto whom all will is spoken,

unto whom nothing is hidden,

I beseech Thee

To cleanse the intent of my heart

With the unspeakable gift of Thy grace

That I may perfectly love Thee

And worthily praise Thee.

Amen.

The Chalice Prayer

Traditional

"Father to Thee I raise my whole being,
a vessel emptied of self.
Accept, Lord, this my emptiness,
and so fill me with Thyself,
Thy Light, Thy Love, Thy Life,
that these Thy precious gifts
may radiate through me
and overflow the chalice of my heart
into the hearts of all
whom I may contact this day,
revealing unto them the beauty
of Thy Joy and Wholeness,
and the serenity of Thy Peace,
which nothing can destroy."

Grace

Reshad Feild

For the food we eat

And the water we drink,

For the wonders of the earth,

the sea and the sky,

For the sun and the rain

and the moon and the stars,

For the early morning

and the evening time,

For Thy love shown
in the Brotherhood of Man,

For all these blessings

and for so many more,

We thank Thee, Father.

Amen.

Grace

J.G. Bennett

All life is one

and everything that lives is holy:

Plants, animals and men.

All must eat to live

and to nourish one another.

We bless the lives

that have died to give us food.

Let us eat consciously,

resolving by our work to pay

the debt of our own existence.

Eight Precepts

Abdulhalik Gudjduvani

1. *Hush der dem*. Be present at every breath. Do not let your attention wander for the duration of a single breath. Remember yourself always and in all situations.

2. *Nazar ber kadem.* Keep your intention before you at every step you take. You wish for freedom and you must never forget it.

3. *Safar der vatan*. Your journey is towards your homeland. Remember that you are traveling from the world of appearances to the world of Reality.

4. *Halvat der endjuman.* In all your outward activity remain inwardly free. Learn not to identify yourself with anything whatsoever.

5. *Yad gerd.* Remember your Friend, i.e. God. Let the prayer of your tongue (*zikr*) be the prayer of your heart (*q'alb*).

6. *Baz gasht.* Return to God. No aim but to attain Reality.

7. *Nigah dasht.* Struggle with all alien thoughts. Keep your mind on what you are doing whether outwardly or inwardly.

8. *Yad dasht.* Be constantly aware of the quality of the Divine Presence. Become used to recognizing the presence of God in your heart.

Prayer of an Anonymous Samurai

14th Century

I have no parents;
I make the heavens and earth my parents.

I have no home;
I make awareness my home.

I have no life or death;
I make the tides of breathing my life and
  death.

I have no divine power;
I make honesty my divine power.

I have no means;
I make understanding my means.

I have no magic secrets;
I make character my magic secret.

I have no body;
I make endurance my body.

I have no eyes;
I make the flash of lightning my eyes.

I have no ears;
I make sensibility my ears.

I have no limbs;
I make promptness my limbs.

I have no strategy;
I make "unshadowed by thought" my
strategy.

I have no designs;
I make "seizing opportunity by the
forelock" my design.

I have no miracles;
I make right-action my miracles.

I have no principles;
I make adaptability to all circumstances
my principles.

I have no tactics;
I make emptiness and fullness my tactics.

I have no talents;
I make ready wit my talent.

I have no friends;
I make my mind my friend.

I have no enemy;
I make carelessness my enemy.

I have no armor;
I make benevolence and righteousness my
armor.

I have no castle;
I make immovable-mind my castle.

I have no sword;
I make absence of self my sword.

The Prayer of Abandonment

Hesychast Fathers

Father, into Thy hands I abandon myself.

Do with me whatever You will, and whatever You do,

I will thank You and remain always grateful.

Let only Thy will be done in me as in all Your creatures.

Into Thy hands, I commit my spirit.

I give it to You with all the love of my heart,

For I love You, Lord,

And so long to give myself with a trust beyond all measure.

Three Prayers

Rabia of Basea

O my Lord, whatever share of this world Thou dost bestow on me, bestow it on Thine enemies, and whatever share of the next world Thou dost give to me, give it to Thy friends. Thou art enough for me.

O my Lord, if I worship Thee from fear of Hell, burn me in Hell, and if I worship Thee from hope of Paradise, exclude me thence, but if I worship Thee for Thine own sake then withhold not from me Thine Eternal Beauty.

O my Lord, the stars are shining and the eyes of men are closed, and kings have shut their doors, and every lover is alone with his beloved...

And here I am alone with Thee.

Mevlana's Prayer

Mevlana Jelaluddin Rumi

Oh, Our Lord God,
I breathe but for Thee,
and I stretch forth my spirit towards Thee
commemorating Thee frequently.

Oh, Our Lord God,
lay not on me an ailment that may make
me forgetful to commemorate Thee,
or lessen my yearning towards Thee,
or cut off the delight I experience
in reciting the litanies of Thy praise.

Grant me not a health
that may engender or increase in me
presumptuous or thankless insolence.

For Thy Mercy's sake,
Oh Thou,
Most Merciful of the Compassionate.

Amen.

Part Three

THE WAY OF MEVLANA

Reshad Feild

Athousand and one questions arise in people's hearts and minds when the subject of Sufism comes up. I am asked such questions as, "Do you have to be a Moslem in order to understand Sufism?" or, "Have you yourself embraced Islam?" Christians ask me whether I believe in Christ. Moslems ask me if I accept the Prophet Mohammed. And still others ask me whether I believe in any form whatsoever. I have received letters filled with threats in one day's mail and filled with thanks in another. There are still people in the world who feel that they can "own" God or impose their personal opinions about God. And yet there are others who have come to know the inner meaning of the words, *Hu Dost* — *He,* that is, the God beyond all conceptual thinking, *is the only Friend.*

Mevlana Jelaluddin Rumi was born on the 30th of September, 1207, and died on the 17th of December, 1273. St. Francis of Assisi was already preaching when Rumi was a child, and it was a time when there was widespread reaction in Europe against the rigid formalism of the Church. The time was ripe for there to be a true taste of the freedom that is found in recognition of the Universal Truth.

Mevlana's "seat" was in Asia Minor, an area

that could almost be seen to be the spiritual hub of the world at that time. It was the perfect place for Rumi to live and extend his influence throughout the world. Even during his lifetime he was accepted, as he is today, as one of the greatest Sufi poets and mystics of all time. Most important of all, Rumi was a human being whose degree of gnosis both embraced all forms of religion and, at the same time, rose above them. In his words, "I am neither Christian nor Jew nor Gabr nor Moslem; my place is the placeless, my trace is the traceless." In many ways he defied logical reasoning. His critics were many and yet it was surely the power of his almost overwhelming love and respect that made him stand above the heads of the theologians.

Afzal Iqbal writes in *The Life and Work of Rumi*:

> Rumi was respected because he respected others. He was considerate even towards his enemies. He was no bigot. Petty differences of creed did not upset him. He always stood for tolerance and toleration. It was well-nigh impossible to provoke him. Nothing could irritate him to anger. One day as he was in a deep mood of contemplation a drunkard walked in shouting and stumbling. As he advanced towards Rumi, he fell on him. His intrusion was serious enough, but to have physically fallen on a saint in his contemplative moments was a crime for which no punishment was severe enough. Rumi's disciples rose as one man and were about to rush at the intruder when the Master waved his hand

and rebuked them gently. "I had thought," said he, "that the intruder was drunk, but now I see that it is not he but my own disciples who are drunk." Wasn't it for this love and consideration even for the most unworthy members of society that he won their unflinching admiration and respect? Wasn't it because of this regard for the meanest of men that he became their unquestioned leader? It is quite easy to understand the devotion of Rumi's admirers who, while he lay on his bier and was washed by the hands of a loving and beloved disciple, did not allow a drop to fall on the ground and drank it as holy water. Nor is it difficult to understand the warmth of feeling with which men of every creed and color-Muslims, Christians, Jews, Arabs and Persians, Turks and Romans-flocked to his funeral procession and smote their breast and rent their garments.

God, in His infinite mercy and compassion, is our daily reminder of *Hu Dost*. At certain times of history, when the moral values have almost disappeared, and at the same time, infinite possibilities seem to lie within our grasp, He brings us special messengers to once again, remind us of His Love. Mevlana was indeed one of these men and today that message is surely as pertinent as it was over 700 years ago.

What is our direct responsibility at this time of history? We stand on the threshold of one of the greatest breakthroughs in human understanding of all time. We are offered the free choice of taking that plunge into the as-yet unknown, or remaining as we are, almost totally immersed in the grips of materialism and the loss of moral values. The great mystics can lead us to view the pyramid of evolution not merely from its apex but from *beyond* its apex. It is there that we can understand the unfoldment of the one Universal Truth throughout time. From this vantage point the six major religions can be seen as containers and distributors of both the laws that govern our lives on earth and the laws that we need to obey in order to know the One Cause behind the apparent causes in the phenomenal world. It is the Breath of God's Compassion that gives us life, and it is the breath of the true mystic that turns the world.

Mevlana is known as the Pole of Love, and Love is "anchored" in Knowledge. That is why, in this school, we also make a study of Muhyiddin Ibn al-'Arabi, the very great Sufi, who is known as the Pole of Knowledge. Ibn 'Arabi, who wrote an enormous number of books, is often referred to as the Doctor Maximus of medieval Europe, as well as the Great Shaykh of the Sufi tradition. The knowledge he gives us is as applicable today as it was 700 years ago.

Ibn 'Arabi lived around the same time as Rumi and they met when Rumi was a young man. It was after meeting Rumi and his father, who was also an influential Shaykh of the time, that Ibn 'Arabi remarked, "There goes a sea followed by an ocean." As perhaps the greatest metaphysician the world has ever known, the study of the works of Ibn 'Arabi is a tremendously exciting adventure. Much of what Arabi expressed in his mystical language 700 years ago is just beginning to be explained by the astrophysicists of today. Indeed it is Knowledge that anchors Love.

Love and Knowledge also need a third aspect of the One Unity to manifest what is necessary for the transition into the next cycle. This aspect we call the Pole of Power. It is represented by Abdul Qadir Gilani, from whose influence the Qadiri Order of Dervishes was started.

Real power comes through complete submission and obedience to the laws of God. God is our Friend and wants to protect us from going astray and falling off the razor's edge road of Truth. He gives us free choice, but the real power that lies within total conviction comes from obedience and the acceptance of authority from the Highest. Abdul Qadir Gilani provides us with no compromise.

So now we have Love, Knowledge and Power, viewed in an intelligent way for all those who wish to understand. In Love there is joy, in Knowledge there is freedom, and in the acceptance of God's laws given to us in His commandments there is Truth.

In the Way of Mevlana we try to live by the example sent to us by the great mystics, and yet adapting ourselves to the changing circumstances. We understand that there are Universal laws which will never change and standards of living which need to always be followed. Forms will come and go, and life in this world is ever-changing, but Love and Knowledge and Power will always be woven together by God, the Great Weaver. As it is said, "Hold fast to the rope of God."

LISTEN TO THE REED

Mevlana Jelaluddin Rumi

In the Name of God the Merciful, the Compassionate.

Listen to the reed how it tells a tale, complaining of separations —

Saying, "Ever since I was parted from the reed-bed, my lament hath caused man and woman to moan.

I want a bosom torn by severance, that I may unfold the pain of love-desire.

Every one who is left far from his source wishes back the time when he was united with it.

In every company I uttered my wailful notes, I consorted with the unhappy and with them that rejoice.

Every one became my friend from his own opinion; none sought out my secrets from within me.

My secret is not far from my plaint, but ear and eye lack the light whereby it should be apprehended.

Body is not veiled from soul, nor soul from body, yet none is permitted to see the soul."

This noise of the reed is fire, it is not wind: whoso hath not this fire, may he be naught!

'Tis the fire of Love that is in the reed, 'tis the fervor of Love that is in the wine.

The reed is the comrade of every one who has been parted from a friend: Its strains pierced our hearts.

Who ever saw a poison and antidote like the reed? Who ever saw a sympathizer and a longing lover like the reed?

The reed tells of the Way full of blood and recounts stories of the passion of Majnun.

Only to the senseless is this sense confided: The tongue hath no customer save the ear.

In our woe the days of life have become untimely: Our days travel hand in hand with burning griefs.

If our days are gone, let them go! — 'tis no matter. Do Thou remain, for none is holy as Thou art!

Whoever is not a fish becomes sated with His water; whoever is without daily bread finds the day long.

None that is raw understands the state of the ripe: Therefore my words must be brief.

Farewell!

LET US GO TOWARD UNION

Ibn al-'Arabi

Listen, O dearly beloved!

I am the reality of the world, the center of the circumference,

I am the parts and the whole.

I am the will established between Heaven and Earth,

I have created perception in you only in order to be the object of my perception.

If then you perceive me, you perceive yourself.

But you cannot perceive me through yourself.

It is through my eyes that you see me and see yourself,

Through your eyes you cannot see me.

Dearly beloved!

I have called you so often and you have not heard me.

I have shown myself to you so often and

you have not seen me.

I have made myself fragrance so often,
and you have not smelled me,

Savorous food, and you have not tasted
me.

Why can you not reach me through the
object you touch

Or breathe me through sweet perfumes?

Why do you not see me? Why do you not
hear me?

Why? Why? Why?

For you my delights surpass all other
delights,

And the pleasure I procure you surpasses
all other pleasures.

For you I am preferable to all other good
things,

I am Beauty, I am Grace.

Love me, love me alone.

Love yourself in me, in me alone.

Attach yourself to me,

No one is more inward than I.

Others love you for their own sakes,

I love you for yourself.

And you, you flee from me.

Dearly beloved!

You cannot treat me fairly,

For if you approach me,

It is because I have approached you.

I am nearer to you than yourself,

Than your soul, than your breath.

Who among creatures

Would treat you as I do?

I am jealous of you over you,

I want you to belong to no other,

Not even to yourself.

Be mine, be for me as you are in me,

Though you are not even aware of it.

Dearly beloved!

Let us go toward Union.

And if we find the road

That leads to separation,

We will destroy separation.

Let us go hand in hand.

Let us enter the presence of Truth.

Let it be our judge

And imprint its seal upon our union

Forever.

DIE BEFORE YOU DIE

Reshad Feild

When you die, and we're all going to die, you carry with you two things — preferably only one, but normally two. The first is everything you think you need, and the second is the knowledge that you have at that moment which is who you are, which is the unique aspect of God. If you know of the unity of God, there is no reincarnation. That's why in *The Last Barrier*, when I asked my teacher, "Is there such a thing as reincarnation?" he said, "Do you really want to know, can you face it?" I couldn't have faced it before, and I'm not saying we can all face it now, but reincarnation is dependent only upon the needs we still think we have in this world. Thinking we need anything is an illusion.

And so you might ask, "Well, what happens then, if I die, do I go on?" And my reply is that you were here from the beginning of time. It's neither going on, nor going back, nor going up, nor going down. Death is the great illusion; death and conception are the same moment; and all creation is in one moment and always has been in one moment.

Now suppose we're going to die in life. We're going for the big one. And by this I mean every single moment of our lives. This also holds true in the so-called physical death. What you carry through death is anything you think you need and everything that you know you are. And the latter is dependent on the lack or loss of the former. Every single moment we give up any idea that we need anything in this life, brings us, God willing, to the point whereby we have some knowledge of the truth of all life.

I can't talk about being dead, because I'm not dead. But I can say what it means to be on your death bed because I've been there twice. I can say, that it is a frustrating thing at that moment to realize we carry across nothing, and that it is a rather funny thing at that moment to consider that what we take across are needs.

I have sat with many people through death in my life. And without exception of any age, there's been that moment of truth in which there is total peace. In the way of the Sufi, we are working towards dying before we die, but the mind says that is tomorrow, or next year, or after I've been through some sort of school work or done this practice or that practice. But the reality of it is not like that at all. What you take across is basically between two things — what you still think you need in life, and the knowledge of who you are. And the latter, as I've said, is dependent upon the loss of the former. If any of us can wake up in the morning, go to bed at night, sit and meditate, have a meal, see our kids, make love, and yet have no needs anymore — then we have the chance of conscious death.

The French expression for orgasm is *le petit mort,* "the little death," and if we could be like that, then we're doing the Work. We have no need. No need whatsoever. Work each day toward no need.

So lastly, I'd like to say how to die — the answer is giving. The answer is in the word *giving,* and nothing else, no thing else, no other word, no other expression. Only in giving totally will we have no need. Only when we empty ourselves completely, that is the way to learn how to die.

TURNING

Reshad Feild

As the curtain goes up on the play of life, so does the light of God descend to us. Yet so seldom do we see this light. We see only its reflections in the waters of life's shadow play. The stage is set. The curtains go up, one after the other. We watch the play; we sit facing the mirror, yet we do not turn around to face the light itself.

The cave is before us. The shadowy figures move and bend in the wind. Perhaps for a few moments we get a taste of the light when the shadows fall away in-between two thoughts. Then again, the play moves on.

Time spins out a web from the past into the future. We try to flee from it, but are imprisoned, trapped like flies to the honey of time. It is sweet this world of ours. And yet we must turn around. We must turn back to our Source.

We cannot wait forever bent over on this wheel of ever-moving illusion. We must halt; stop for awhile in our tracks. We need to look back once to see where we have come from and then, ever so slowly, turn our backs on the play. It is our home no longer. We turn to our one and only true home, which is the home of the Beloved.

Turning — turning towards the morning of our lives. The day is dawning at last, for now it comes from our real beginning where we have turned not. For so long we thought our beginning was behind us in the distant echoes of the past. Yet this beginning arrives when we have turned our backs on the past, gratefully and wisely, when we have turned from the false security of everything we knew and turn towards our real beginning.

This is our true birth — the first step we take on the Path of Return. Onwards and onwards we turn back to this eternal beginning of our lives. Joy springs forth in the Light behind the sun. This is the triumphant Sun of suns, the King of kings. This is the beginning of Life everlasting.

Once we thought. Then we did not think. We turned to God, not to the transient shadow world. Once we turned to God, then we turned in God, as He turned Himself in us. We heard the good news, we saw the good news, and we proclaim the good news as we turn back, once more, to His Creation. Separation is dissolved in Unity. God and His Creation are finally seen as One. We turn and world turns back to Him. He is pleased as He receives His beloved servants. He smiles as we smile. He glorifies as we glorify. We are in Him as He is in us. We die to the shadows and are reborn in the Light of Truth. We die in the Light of Truth and are reborn in the Light of Essence. And, we die in the Light of Essence, for we know there is only

He through whose masquerade the world was born.

> *"I was a hidden treasure and I loved to be known; so I created the world that I might be known."*

> — *Hadith of the Prophet Muhammed*

Reason is powerless in the expression of Love.

Love alone is capable of revealing the truth of Love and being a Lover.

The way of our prophets is the way of Truth.

If you want to live, die in Love.

Die in Love if you want to remain alive.

— Mevlana Jelaluddin Rumi

About The Author

The life story of Dr. Reshad Feild reads like a modern-day Odyssey propelled by the single question, *"What is the purpose of Life on Earth?"*

Reshad left the aristocratic roots of his native England at an early age having had a mystical experience he describes as "like having a window opened."

His mystical yearning took him around the world to Zen monasteries in Japan, the Himalayas in Nepal, and to the Sufi mystics and the Whirling Dervishes in Turkey. He also studied with the Gurdjieff and Ouspensky schools and the ancient Druids in England.

His life has led him in other directions as well. He has been an antiques dealer, a stockbroker, and a naval officer. In the early sixties Reshad sang with the British pop group, the Springfields.

Throughout the years, Reshad Feild has run several esoteric schools in England, Canada, and the U.S. to help young people embarking on the path of human transformation.

Many of these experiences are recounted in his books which include, *The Last Barrier, The Invisible Way, Steps to Freedom, Here to Heal, The*

Traveling People's Feild Guide, Footprints in the Sand, Breathing Alive, and *The Alchemy of the Heart.*

Reshad Feild works with study groups in Switzerland, Germany, England, Holland, and the United States.